Introduction

This is the story of a bipolar man. My story and my adventures are as magical as they are crazy and chaotic. I'm going to tell you about my many adventures, my discoveries and my journey through the gaps of reality. This illness is as difficult for the sufferer to live with as it is for the outside world to understand. Manic or euphoric states are states of excitement where we feel superhuman, and conversely, depressive states are states of great distress where we feel fallible and subhuman. Without proper treatment, I'd oscillate between these states, living a dark life in my lightless room, or as white as a hospital gown.

For a long time, I refused to accept that I was fragile or mentally ill. I thought, and sometimes I still think, that the events I experienced were not the result of psychic weakness, but rather a message, a mission from a higher power. What could be more normal than to have faith in oneself, even if only for a moment? All this was (seemed) so very, very real.

In a manic crisis, I had the impression of changing, transforming, programming the entire universe and finding the flaw, like a spermatozoon fertilizing the egg, but in this case, the egg was the Earth and the spermatozoon was me. My illness caused me to lose many friends, some of whom weren't really friends at all. In reality, they were just people passing through life, who take advantage of you when you're doing well and abandon you when you're not, the same kind of people who only take healthy animals from pet shops and abandon those who need them most, by the side of the road.

I don't want to hurt people like that. However, I do know that life will put them on the floor of harsh reality sooner or later. And, when that day comes, let no one weep for them to realize the plight of a lonely and seriously injured person in a world such as ours.

I'm now stabilized on Teralithe[1] after having tried a panoply of pills, and after six crises, including five manic ones, and the consequences of such a mess, I presume I can finally follow my studies without putting an end to them any time soon. I therefore hope to be able to achieve my goal of a great education and at last be able to pursue a career in a passionate profession, whatever that may be, since there are so many fields that appeal to me.

---

[1] Basic treatment for bipolar disorders. It is a mood regulator (thymoregulator) whose active ingredient is a lithium salt (♫ Nirvana-Title: Lithium).

Let me introduce myself: my name is Alexandre Bertorello, dark-haired, green-eyed, rather slim and six feet tall, so you can use my diminutive Alex without fear of reprisal. What's more, I was born on October 29, 1994 in Toulon, in the Font Pré hospital, now destroyed. Toulon is the capital of the Var department in southeastern France, with a population of around one hundred and eighty thousand, a Mediterranean harbor often considered the most beautiful in Europe, and the largest military port on the continent.

As I write this, in April 2019, I live in Carnoules, a charming little village in the heart of the Var, with a population of around three thousand five hundred, whose emblem is a locomotive, one of which stands at the entrance to the village. This emblem is no accident, as Carnoules was the largest station between Nice and Marseille before the Second World War. I'm currently living with my grandparents and am therefore 24 years old.

I'm passionate about all areas of life, and especially about love, because I believe that love is the only true quest for our existence on this planet. I love nature and animals, especially birds of prey, which I've always loved. Although I don't have an eagle, I do have a small flock of waved parakeets, which I see on a regular basis. To tell you the truth, I'm currently writing this article against a backdrop of their chirping, close to their aviary. I should also point out that my grandparents' house is an ideal place to find peace and inspiration. With a beautiful view of Our Lady of the Angels[2] .

---

[2] A description of this location will follow.

To conclude and return to the subject of the book, I also live in a land of extremes, for if you haven't already grasped it, I suffer from bipolar disorder type 1. This type of bipolarity is characterized by the presence of one or more manic episodes, with or without major depressive phases. To put it simply, a manic episode is a state of great euphoria, with an exaltation of mood, a feeling of omnipotence and megalomania. This is usually preceded by a phase of hypomania, which is a less intense form of mania, more suited to life in society.

The combination of hypomania and depression is characteristic of people with type 2 bipolar disorder, who do not experience the manic episodes of type 1, and who are therefore much more prone to depression than to euphoria, etc.

Chapter 1
The beginning

As 2013 draws to a close, I've just passed my scientific baccalaureate. I'm happy because I've got a girlfriend, even though my in-laws don't like me much because I smoke with their daughter. It has to be said that nobody except my grandparents made me understand that smoking was a hard drug, just like any other drug, it was so commonplace to smoke, everyone did it and extolled the substance as a medicine that wise people consume to grow intellectually.

But it's all a deception: drugs ride the wave of human distress by providing a refuge for beings, a lure that sends them straight into total amorphism. In short, I had a very complicated childhood, with lots of moves, lots of responsibilities at an early age and parents at war. For six years after my birth, all was well, and I lived in Le Luc en Provence, in our family home. A beautiful village, also in the heart of the Var, with a population of ten thousand three hundred, and a hexagonal tower dominating the village. In short, a well-balanced life with parents who were always there for us. When I was six years old, my brother Elie was born, a normal, growing family. Then one day, when I was eight, my parents decided to move to Spain. I was against it, but what could I do? I was going to lose all my friends and my girlfriend from primary school, to go to a country where I didn't even know the language.

We went there and arrived in our "seaside" studio in La Pineda de Salou, a very touristy town in the province of Tarragona in Catalonia, with fake iron trees lining the beach as its symbol. It's a village on the shores of the

Mediterranean, on the edge of a large industrial zone and a large "Port Aventura" theme park.

My parents had decided that I would take the bus alone to a Franco-Spanish school several kilometers from La Pineda. For the first day, my father, 33 years old and whose first name is Jean-Luc, nicknamed "Lucky" by his friends, accompanied me on this journey, which was so frightening for me at the time. Fortunately, he soon gave up the idea, as it was so complicated for an eight-year-old to take all those buses on his own. He put me in a Spanish school in La Pineda, and every morning and evening I cycled through town and along the beach to get to CE2. Things were going well, I was getting used to life there, I had lots of friends and I had a pretty good command of Spanish. I remember stopping in stores to buy Pokémon cards and Beyblade spinning tops, for those in the know.

At the end of the school year, we moved into a very large village house my father had bought in Riudoms, a village of six thousand six hundred inhabitants and the birthplace of the renowned Catalan architect Antoni Gaudí, builder of Barcelona's Sagrada Familia. Riudoms, a village with its renowned Saint Jaume church from the XVIe century, a magnificent church. After the move, problems arose.

Then, a few months out of school, my parents started arguing. My mother was passionate about witchcraft and fortune-telling, and stayed with some crazy people who told her my father was evil, and so on. My mother already wasn't clear, because I think I inherited that from her, apart from the fact that she never looked after herself.

From there, my mother repatriated my two-year-old brother Elie and me to France for a few months, then they reconciled. We returned to Spain, but the arguments became increasingly violent, and I feared there might be a murder. I was with Elie in the living room and plates were flying, one even grazed his skull and exploded on the stairs.

Frankly, it wasn't a good experience for two children to go through if you don't want them to have problems later on. Finally, our mother picked us up and took us back with her to France, to the starting point in Le Luc en Provence, in an apartment. It was the fifth time I'd changed schools, to the point where the notion of friendship no longer meant anything to me; friends in my definition had become nothing more than passing acquaintances.

In short, my father returned to France and obtained alternating custody, which meant that every other weekend they were at war, hitting each other in the street in front of everyone, our children's breaches were wide open and they continued to deepen them.

To get away from my father, at the end of my CM2, my mother decided to take Elie and me to Reunion Island, a small paradise island, although the tour would soon be completed. We lived in the village of Les Avirons with its eleven-thousand-four-hundred inhabitants, populated by magnificent native plants and trees, above the village of Étang-Salé and its black volcanic sand beaches.

It was the sixth time I had changed schools. This time I arrived at college in 6□,every evening my mother either went out or brought a man home, I'll let you imagine what it does in a child's head to know that his mother is akin to a prostitute. My brother would cry at night when my mother went out, and I would comfort him with my presence.

In the end, being a mother is no guarantee of being a self-respecting adult. For example, I was fed up with her and she was fed up with us, whipping us with her belt as soon as we did something wrong. I also did everything I could to get her to send us back to our father, and that's what she did after my 6□.

So we landed at the dingy airport of France's second-largest city, Marseille in the Bouches-du-Rhône, to live with our grandparents in Carnoules, and it was really cool to get back to our roots. What's more, we no longer lacked anything, we'd had PlayStations, we were happy, the hard times were over.

A psychologist advised my grandmother, whose first name was Marlène, a 72-year-old brunette with brown eyes and curly hair like me, to take me to see a psychiatrist.

Of course, I didn't feel the need to, I felt fine and perfectly adapted. So I told her there was no need, she listened and quickly abandoned the idea of imposing this kind of follow-up on me.

So I went to secondary school on my own, living in a small studio under my grandparents' house in Carnoules, as my father was living in Spain at the time. Then, after passing my "brevet des collèges", I entered the Lycée Jean-Aicard in Hyères Les Palmiers, a beautiful town in the Var, also touristy, with a population of fifty-four thousand, and I lived in my grandmother's family home, which my father had bought in Carnoules. He himself had returned from Spain and was living with his new girlfriend in Gonfaron, also in the heart of the Var and with a population of four thousand. This is my 2□ little brother's mother, her name is Clara.

All this to tell you that by middle school, I was living on my own, and by high school, when I was 15, I was self-sufficient, managing my meals and household chores on my own. My father gave me a weekly allowance, so frankly, I had nothing to complain about. Then, when I was 18, during my final year in science, I traveled with my father to Latin America, to Argentina, but in particular to Paraguay, which was truly paradise, with wonderful people and a climate as humid and warm as the human warmth that reigns there. I enjoyed riding a motorcycle without a helmet, or guiding a herd of cows with a very good "friend" of mine.

What's more, everyone there wants to invite you to spend the evening at their place. So it's very difficult to have to refuse these kind people their hospitality, but since you can't duplicate yourself for these people, I spent my evenings with friends I met in Caacupé. I spent my evenings with friends I'd met in Caacupé, a town of twenty-thousand inhabitants, a major Paraguayan pilgrimage site with its cathedral-basilica of Our Lady of the Miracles.

When I got back, I was so bored with being back in the West that I had to spend at least a week not working on my high school courses. Then I met Anna, a beautiful and very sweet little flower with light brown hair and beautiful blue eyes, who was in the première littéraire and a year younger than me. In short, my first real girlfriend in high school, we spent our days chatting at home, smoking together, and I regularly took her out on my 50cc scooter to nature spots, notably the **Réal Martin river**[3] in Puget-Ville. Puget-Ville is the first rural village east of Toulon with a population of four thousand three hundred, located in the heart of the Var region.

---

[3] Martin: first name of my "best friend" from high school.

That being the case, I passed my scientific baccalaureate without too much trouble, because Anna was my priority, my passion, in short, my first great love. I tried to convince her not to, but no, her parents did everything they could to get her to move back home, and she did, and I suffered enormously, as I do every time I separate.

On October 29, 2013, instead of going straight into Postbac studies, I decided to take a gap year and on my birthday, for my 19th birthday. I received a message on social networks from my mother, whom I hadn't heard from for eight years.

She wanted me to visit her in New Caledonia, which I did, inviting me to her home in Dumbéa, a twin town to Nouméa, the small Kanak capital[4] of ninety-four thousand inhabitants. We often got into a tangle, she was crazy and touchy about the slightest thing I said, I was, according to her, manipulated by my father and his family.

What's more, there was a Buddha statue by the pool which had started to cry from the right eye, and my mother was telling me it was my fault. Luckily, I'd spent the night with some great people in Nouméa who were kind enough to take me in, and she picked me up the next day. In short, I'd had enough, I was bored, it was getting so heavy that she and my father-in-law decided to send me to New Zealand, on the pretext of giving me an adventurous vacation. I understood that they wanted to get rid of me, and I was happy to discover a new country on my own. They paid for my plane ticket and gave me $600 pocket money for ten days, and off I went.

---

[4] The Kanak people are the indigenous French Melanesian people of New Caledonia.

I've never felt so free and happy as I did after this trip, landing in Auckland, which is not the capital but the most populous city in New Zealand's North Island, with over one million five hundred thousand inhabitants and a twelve-hour time difference with France. Knowing that jet lag is one of the reasons, along with conflict, role transition, social isolation and bereavement, that can lead to decompensation, it was perhaps one of the conditions that led me to trigger my first crisis following this journey. I was staying in a backpacker[5] in the city.

I had bought a tent for 5 dollars from a Uruguayan who had finished his trip around the two islands, on the principle of going camping and not finding myself without money. I took the bus to the village of Rotoroa, with its lake and its pungent smell of sulfur, where I stayed one night in a hostel as well. Frankly, it was magnificent to find myself in the land of "Lord of the Rings", the sidewalks were bursting with volcanic activity under the floor and the village was littered with Maori-style houses. Incidentally, I met a Maori boy[6] whom I had taken under my wing, bought breakfast for in the morning and who had taught me to say, my name is Alex in Maori "Ko Alek takou

---

[5] Backpapers" are youth hostels where you can meet people of all ethnicities, especially South Americans, as the continent is quite close to New Zealand.

[6] The Maoris are an indigenous Polynesian people living in New Zealand, and some of them make great rugby players with their All-Blacks national team and their start-of-match choreography, the Haka, which I admire and which reminds me of the dance of death.

ingaoa" and a bunch of other little phrases in case I ended up in a tribe, which however didn't happen.

On December 30, 2013, I packed my bag and headed for Taupo, a town of twenty-five-thousand-four-hundred inhabitants located northeast of a magnificent lake overlooking the Tongariro volcano, or Mordor for connoisseurs of the "Lords of the Rings".

So I spent my New Year's Day partying in Taupo with a sleepless night, which is still a de-synchronizer, incompatible with a good mental health lifestyle. But, hey, when you're young, well, it's the last thing on your mind to have a good vital rhythm, especially on a special day like New Year's Day and in a country completely on the Western side of the World.

So the next day, the first day of 2014, I set off with my bag and tent into the wilderness above Taupo, and the real adventure had begun. I hiked randomly along trails until I found a hot spring on the banks of the Waikato River, where I took my 30-degree bath. I chatted at length with an American woman, a very interesting mother, and then continued on my way for about ten kilometers, until I landed at a public campsite where I hurriedly pitched my tent.

The sun was beginning to disappear and I had eaten my cans of tuna. There were a multitude of gnats in my beautiful $5 blue abode, but that didn't worry me; after all, gnats aren't mosquitoes, so I fell asleep like an anvil. The next day, I woke up with "tons" of red patches on my body; in truth, the bugs I'd mistaken for midges were called "sandflies", nothing more than a plague insect of New Zealand that like mosquitoes sucks your blood and makes you itch afterwards. In short, it was a very pleasant wake-up call. I never complain, so it's okay, I left my tent. I then reversed my route to take my bath at the hot spring early in the morning. It's so nice! After enjoying this tantalizing moment, I set off to visit Huka Falls. These are very violent falls, with some crazy people in canoes and kayaks going over them, so it's pretty impressive.

The following day, I visited the "Craters of the Moon", a truly magical place with intense volcanic activity and boiling sulphur and water holes where the Maoris cooked their food; really, it was top-notch.

Nine days had passed unexpectedly, so I had to get ready to go back to my mother in New Caledonia. I reluctantly did so, and headed back to Auckland airport in the direction of Nouméa. Back at my mother's, I waited for the time to pass as it had before the trip to the Maoris, until it was time for me to return to France. When I got home, I started smoking regularly and shut myself away in a bubble. I'd been through so much all at once that the pressure inside me was building...

Chapter 2
The divine crisis

The pressure was mounting, all I could do was write tons of bits of sentences on social networks, whatever came into my head, I couldn't sleep, couldn't eat, I was realizing my passion, thinking and sharing. What guided me was love, I wanted to find my princess, the one who would wipe away my tears, I still loved Anna. I was also caught up in these sort of delirious flushes, thinking I was the Chosen One, the little prince perched on the moon. I was so sad and lonely that I embellished all that and decorated my life with fantasy, a great distress call to the universe. Suddenly, I received a stream of energy from the sky to my skull, making a continuous "vrouwww" inside my head. There was a girl two years my junior, Camille, a beautiful, petite Venusian creature with red hair and green eyes, who lived in Carnoules like me. She came to talk to me on social networks and I immediately thought she was coming to deliver a message. I was in my own world and when I spoke to her, it was as if she was responding to my delusions and reinforcing them, whereas in reality, this wasn't the case at all. In my imagination, I wasn't talking to Camille, but to Mother Nature.

Initially, it was like a battle between my blue masculine energy from Father Sky and his menstrual red feminine energy from Mother Earth, I was protected by the flow of energy that was "given" to me.

I was already crazy about her, and really thought she was this goddess of nature. In my universe, she told me she was imprisoned in matter as if by a curse. So I wanted to free her, my wife, the mother goddess, and me, the man, the father of heaven. I wanted to conquer the world in her presence, but all I wanted above all was her love, which I imagined would anaesthetize all my suffering.

This suffering created by my abyssal wounds that only hypersensitive beings can know, an evil dug into her existence and most fearsome. My desire to sleep had totally disappeared, three nights without sleep and the last day, day turned into night instantly, Camille didn't answer me anymore, Mother Nature was forced in her world to cut off all communication with me, I was crazy, crazy about her, but also crazy about them, about all the female figures I'd more or less fallen for, even if my greatest weakness was her, it was Camille.

So I got on my scooter and set off in search of the truth. I wanted to find answers, as I was in the throes of an intellectual mess and completely incoherent. At the time, my delirium was in its infancy, chaotic and without any finesse. I wanted to know which girl had enabled me to speak to my goddess from beyond the earth through Camille, and which one was the relay. I thought of Anna, that famous Camille and Noémie, with whom I was chatting on Facebook. Each had different eyes: blue, green and black. I associated the three colors with the powers of a female trio destined to bring me a message from the beyond, and I thought that these three girls who had had a relationship with me had the mission of guiding me, the chosen one of the goddess "Hylia", goddess of the sky "the Blessed Virgin", I was Link[7] and I was looking for Zelda the princess.

[7] Link: hero of the Japanese game "The Legend of Zelda", which translates as "link" in English.

By scooter, I went to Anna's village, Pierrefeu, a village watered by the Real Martin like "a rock" in the middle of Hyères, Puget-ville, Collobrières and Cuers in the Toulon Provence Méditerranée metropolitan area. I searched for her everywhere, climbed over gates, talked to people she knew who guided me to her, and finally found her surrounded by her friends. They pushed me away from her, she fled to her parents' house, and as I only wanted to talk to her, her parents blocked my way, grabbed their phone and called the police.

They put me in their Kangoo and took me to their headquarters. There was a gendarmette with blue eyes like Anna's, I thought she must be giving me a message, so I chased her into the gendarmerie and she laughed, my father arrived angry. I didn't want to go back to him, so the gendarmes called the fire department, who put me in their truck and took me to hospital. When they arrived, they told me "you can leave here now or go into hospital", at first I wanted to leave, but in my delirium I decided to go into hospital, I thought it was about following my prophetic path, so I went in, they tied me to a bed at all four ends hands and feet tied to the edges of the bed.

It was a horrible feeling, but I thought it was a test, a crucifixion, I had become Jesus and the white sheet on my hospital bed represented my Turin shroud. After much shouting in my hospital cell, the doctor came with some nurses who gave me an injection, which plunged me into the torpor of a sleep of nothingness.

When I woke up, I was in my underpants in a room, full of IVs, I can't say how long I'd been asleep. I tore everything off and got out of bed, and when I found myself in some corridors, a nurse saw me almost naked and came to escort me back to my room, telling me to get dressed.

That was it: at the end of August 2014, I'd landed in a psychiatric ward, but that didn't mean I'd come back down to Earth... it was the first time I'd been sequestered, and as I mentioned, I was in the middle of a mission. I saw the healing body as the one that wanted to deprive me of my dreams, of my progress towards enlightenment.

I spent my days writing poems, hoping to change people's minds - it was a real battle. I loved talking to certain psychiatrists; they had the light bulb over their heads and understood my illness. There was one in particular who was very calm and kind, even though I was far out in the stratosphere. He read my writings and poems, and to calm my anger, tried to lower my medication as I requested, even though in the end I never took it, hiding the pills under my tongue and spitting them out. As for me, what I remembered about the medication was the syllable "lie".

I was creating tension between the nurses, some of whom couldn't tolerate the fact that I didn't have much medication to take, while others said nothing. One day, they increased my medication and I took it. I then faked fainting, to make it look as if the medication was too strong, so that I wouldn't take any more. Andrea, a bedside colleague, now deceased from drug overdose, saw me falling to the floor and called the nurses, they took me to the consultation bed and, of course, my simulation hadn't worked, in any case, I noticed a difference between them, some laughed, others got angry and the last ones had a lot of pain that I could see on their faces. I particularly remember Vincent, to whom I dedicated a poem, in which I played on his first name, his kindness, his air of innocence and compassion, which he evoked in me, unlike the other nurses, who were less empathetic and more authoritarian. I don't have the poem any more, though; I've written a lot of them, and they've all ended up in oblivion. Although I write them often, I don't want to archive them.

It was finally the day of my release, having played the cured patient game well, I was finally released, but the beast that was gnawing at me continued to do so. I saw signs everywhere, I read license plate numbers; the numbers and letters communicated a message to me, it was a sign, a sign from her, the one I love, my desired one, the one destined for me.

I was now convinced it was Camille, so I set my sights on her, spoke to her again and suggested an outing, which she accepted. I took her to the summit of the Maures at Notre Dame des Anges in Pignans, a fantastic spot of nature populated by chestnut trees perched at the top of the Maures range at an altitude of 780 meters, with a chapel and an antenna, all by scooter. We chatted a lot, she didn't even smoke pot with me, she was perfect in my eyes, then her mother must have been worried about her being with me and she and her boyfriend told her to go home then. I got her on my scooter and took her back to the road where her parents picked her up, so when I think back on it the poor thing...

The second time we saw each other and kissed, I was really in love, but there was one obstacle between us, and that was the friendship of her best friend who wouldn't let her go. We went to sleep at my house and I kissed her all night long. It was great, but because I'm a little crazy I misinterpret things, I was going to start doing more than kissing, which she didn't like at all and so she went home.

In the end, I didn't like her mate and the influence she had on Camille, like all crazy friendships for that matter.

Anyway, I went back to see her, only this time it was to go with some friends of hers to some kind of concert in Hyères. In short, all I wanted was to be alone with Camille, so the pain and frustration reawakened the evil in me and I plunged back into crisis, ridicule and madness...

I'll let you imagine the judgment Camille must have had on me, I was so angry with myself. On the one hand, I knew I was fooling around, on the other, I wanted to add fuel to the flames and fool around even more, but this side of me won the game and slowly the fire grew...

Chapter 3
The primitive crisis

Since then, I'd been staying with my grandparents, under their supervision, in a villa in the remote countryside of the village, spending my days doing nothing. My first crisis had caused me to miss my entry into the first year of medical school (PACES) at the University of Montpellier.

I refused to take my medication, and then everyone but my grandmother thought I wasn't ill, that it was just a late-onset teenage crisis. So I didn't take any medication, but my delusions were there and I tried to hide them, but my brain was working, imagining a whole world. I dreaded every mystical symbol. I wrote and wrote.

Work, always as if it were the only possible source of happiness, the only one in any case that could fulfill my dream of greatness, of entering the rift and joining my goddess, I was convinced of being supreme, of being the king of the anthill that is this insignificant and absurd humanity. I used to hide to smoke, which my grandparents didn't tolerate at all.

My heartache had been amplified by my obsession with Camille to the point where I was fixated on her and didn't want to talk to me anymore, although I can understand that, because I was shot.

I began my mystical ritual, sitting on my bed in front of my PC. I'd string together sentences, words, sometimes numbers, and it would make sense to others, sometimes not at all. What's certain is that I understood everything I was doing, and everything I was doing made sense in a way that I, the person writing to you today, being stabilized, can't even begin to understand.

Everything that came out of my mind, out of the chasms, out of hell, was the rejection of the flames inside me, it bubbled up. As it will always bubble, so much hatred, anger, violence resides in these lands, that when you open the doors as I did, everything burns, everything annihilates and putrefies; there is no more beauty, no more kindness, no more gentleness, there is only the evil one. Heaven and hell are within us, rest assured.

I went back to not sleeping or eating, staying up late and worrying my grandparents. After the third sleepless night, the dreams began to come alive and blend with reality. I was writing, listening to music (especially rap) and the more mystical the sounds, the more they resonated with me. It was as if the singers were speaking on my behalf, whatever they were saying, they were singing to converse about my life, their sufferings were the same as mine and their poetry came from God, hence from me...

As I said, everything was there to communicate a message to me. I didn't hear any voices, but I associated what I saw with the message from my "imaginary" beloved. It must have been late at night, I was with my little dog, Terri, when I read a publication with a photo of a dog asking "please give me some food". I took one look at my dog Terri and he was asking me that, in my head, he was hungry so I got up, went to the fridge room and emptied the contents of the fridge on the floor for him. My grandmother came in, I was totally delirious, she screamed in anger, I only said weird things that only I understood, my grandfather, whose first name was Jean-Pierre, arrived and didn't understand either. He tried to frighten me with a stick and threw a blow at me, so I protected my face with an Age-Uke, a karate protection technique. It was as if everything I'd learned suddenly came in handy.

I escaped into the countryside surrounding my grandparents' villa, stripping off all my clothes. I also went to the hill behind their house, wanting to get back to nature, to purify myself by returning to the primitive stage, which I did, I took a dirt track and followed it all the way. I climbed the wild, thorny hillside barefoot, my feet bleeding, I heard noises, probably wild boars. I shouted at them, thinking they were the vermin of darkness.

It was nighttime and I knew of a cave, or rather a small rift at the top of this hill (which actually exists), so I went there and settled in. The crevice is a little deep and warm, and my astrological sign is Scorpio, so I lay down on the ground like an insect among the spiders and their webs. At that moment, I felt extremely alive and free, hundreds of times better than any state a normal person can find themselves in having taken substances or not.

I watched the cave exit as I lay on the floor. I waited, thinking I was going to be sucked into the depths of the Earth and follow my destiny into Hell, but nothing of the sort happened, my brain was at 2000. I also saw, through the cave entrance, night turning into day and back into night in a matter of minutes, the kind of delirium that reinforces the psychosis I was in.

I stepped out of the cave, thinking I'd changed dimensions, it was still dark, I stood at the entrance and saw five lights in the sky in the distance. They were very slow and not so far from the ground, approaching in my direction. Halfway down the path leading to the top of the hill, the lights advanced and I looked up: they were five triangular vessels of white light. I thought they were coming to get me; they flew right over me. I then realized that they couldn't be airplanes, especially since the Patrouille de France doesn't go on parade at this hour, and that they were far too slow and too close not to make noise and be airplanes. They flew over me and went away until I couldn't see them anymore.

I went down into the undergrowth and saw a wall of light in the small dirt path, like luminous balls advancing towards me. In my mind, they were angels, but I didn't want to take the easy way out, which was to go straight to heaven. They came forward and I hid in the brambles so they wouldn't meet me. I wanted to finish the mission I'd set myself on Earth, I didn't want to reach heaven and disappear without difficulty.

Then I got thirsty, and the one thing I could never get rid of in my crises was the need to drink. It was like Michel Fugain's song "fait comme l'oiseau...", living on love and fresh water. For me, it was the key to the survival of the human species, to putting an end to the murder of animal species and getting in touch with the Superior. The goal was enlightenment, to be creatures of light feeding on water and love alone. The wall of light had disappeared, and I got up, still naked, to return to my grandparents' house with an enormous thirst. There were vines along the way, and to drink, I sucked the grapes, the blood of Christ, my blood. Yes, because in my case, I was all-in-one, all the gods, all the great prophets, all the dead, I was the one who single-handedly represented all beliefs and even worse, everything that existed. I was the one sent and God himself.

Back home, my grandmother didn't want to open the door, she was afraid, so she called my father and finally opened it. In the meantime, I had (throw) the pump of a pond to my grandfather to empty it and return the water to the earth, everything from then on was symbolic. My father arrived, sternly calmed me down and took me to his house, where I settled on a folding mattress in the room. I couldn't sleep. I didn't want to. I put sound on my mobile and the next day my father had to go to work when the sun came up. I was alone and as delirious as ever, I turned on the taps all over the house and my father arrived in a huff. I threw his keys in the garbage can and fled over the roof. I climbed over the railings of the neighboring houses and ended up in the big field behind the house. I walked to the little river and climbed down.

Once in the riverbed, I removed all my belongings and clothes and, going upstream against the current, I removed all the pumps from the nearby houses that were taking water from the river. I wanted to give water back to the planet, there was no way I was going to let mankind monopolize it. Once again, I climbed through the undergrowth, following the path of shadows made by tree branches and electric wires on the ground. I climbed like a monkey. I followed the shadow trail until I landed in the garden of a house with a swimming pool; this was my final destination and I dived in. The owners saw me and called the gendarmes, all the while being very disturbed, which I can understand, a naked guy in their house (it's the asylum coming to the house, I think it's funny). They gave me a towel to cover myself, and the gendarmes arrived to take me home in their blue Kangoo with sirens, as they always do.

Again, I gave false addresses, I didn't want to go home. Once again, day turned to night as we passed through the village of Pierrefeu, just before the town of Hyères, where the emergency room is located. Through the windows of the gendarmerie car, I saw the village center as if at war, women crying, being beaten by the military, young people being commandeered in army trucks. What can I say, it was like one of Hitler's big war movies, with the army in charge, the sun shining and the rain pouring down on the civilians?

All this reinforced my delirium, which I lived through very well and pleasantly at the time. The gendarmes laughed with me, and one pretended to be Captain America. In the car, the control unit said there was a man with an axe who wanted to kill another person. It sounded so delirious that it reinforced my trip, I said that this man was surely a good man for humor and the gendarmes were delirious with me. On the freeway, they were driving very fast and there was a speed camera at the entrance to Hyères. The gendarmes told me to give them the finger for the photo, and I was thrilled, so I didn't hesitate to do so until I was flashed in their car! In any case, I really enjoyed it and would have loved to have seen the photo with my own eyes.

Then they took me to the hospital, and again, the nurses tied me up as usual. This time, however, I ended up in intensive care psychiatry at the Pierrefeu aux Palmiers 1 hospital. I woke up in a room, still completely delirious. I met a woman, Sandy, a beautiful blonde in her thirties, who lived in La Garde, a town with a population of twenty-five thousand, and some other friends; I assigned each of them a role in a card game; I was all the cards, especially the joker, and I valued the best by assigning them the position of king or queen. Some were happy with the place I gave them, and others who had numbers like five rather than trumps were unhappy about it.

I used to write a lot, and I remember one particular sick discovery: when we link our hands with our fingers, our hand lines form the word ALLA, like the Muslim God. So, as I loved playing with words, I modelled my first name and Alexandre became Al(exe)lA where Alex is written in mirror image, giving "Alex est là" or AllA.

I was good at computers and .exe means executable for software, so I was an envoy (software) to transform the world. I immediately shared my discovery with everyone. However, no one but the patients gave any importance to it, which partly brought me down. I spent my time taking refuge in love, and as a result, I kissed and cuddled Sandy, even though she was eleven years older than me, I saw her as a goddess.

All this is exhausting, the brain is in turmoil and the descent is like a war with oneself. You don't want to give in to reality, even if everything tells you you're wrong, you cling to your beautiful imagination, you don't want to be part of the world again. I came out of psychiatry for the second time and my father didn't understand me then, he started blaming me, telling me I was useless, that I didn't even have a flat at my age; for him. I wasn't sick, just having a teenage crisis.

Chapter 4
The crisis of royalty

I was released from psychiatry again, and this time I was still in my normal state for a month or two. I didn't stay at my grandparents', I used to go and smoke joints almost every night at Tonio's, a very tall, dark-haired outsider and former friend of my father, who also thought it was just an adolescent crisis.

I still refused to take my medication, and what's more, when I did take it, it gave me a whole host of side effects. I kept writing until I was back in my trance state. I was out of my mind again. I got on my scooter and headed for Pignans, the neighboring village of three thousand nine hundred inhabitants, where the famous Notre Dame des Anges to the south of the village dominates.

I was standing in the school square, with a large water fountain depicting a hunter (Jules Gérard) surrounded by lions, water that was not drinkable, I was thirsty, I drank the water coming out of the mouth of the fountain's lion statue, the sun was gradually going down as it set. I kept staring at it, trying to make it rise again, and I had the impression that it was working, that it remained frozen. I was concentrating on getting it back to its zenith, when I saw a person in a wheelchair. Both his legs were amputated. In my mind, I was there to make amends for God's mistakes in leaving man, his creation, sick and disabled. I talked with him and told him who I was: God in other words. I'd talk to him about all sorts of things and tell him about my deepest belief, that the spirit transforms matter, what we call faith. I wanted him to stand up and think so hard about legs, I wanted to give him the saving hope that makes the impossible possible.

I entered his skull like a great illusionist or manipulator, call it what you will. We were both laughing, my words were like bread and butter to him. He had so much faith in me that he pretended to get up and walk, but it didn't work, even I in my delusional role knew it wasn't going to work. I let him go with his wheelchair with the promise that one day, I would cure the evil of all mankind, including his own, because I believed I needed time to understand things in order to act effectively.

It's completely crazy, I know, but as someone who lived through it, it was a moment of great emotion and intense compassion. I went to the village church and forced my way in. I was alone inside, I sat down at the front and put all my belongings on the altar as if for a ritual, I lit the candles. I was at home in my temple, starting up my laptop with music. I danced too, I was at 100,000, I was talking to myself, and as I conversed with myself, I had the intimate conviction that she could hear me.

Yes. She, my beloved imprisoned under matter, for she had confided in me that she saw exactly everything but could not act. So I began to act as if she were with me, I took on the governance of the world with her. She was present in this ecclesiastical silence, and when I got thirsty, I drank like a bear from the basin of holy, blessed water. I was ecstatic with the candles and paintings that were my crowning glory. I'd finally become king of the world, and the church's unoccupied seats were, for me, in my delirious omnipotence, well and truly occupied by crowds of spirits, of the invisible dead.

I was making my speech in front of all these people who didn't exist, but without seeing them, I imagined (not hallucinated) them looking at me and listening to me. I felt their presence, they were in my mental construct, moved, proud of me and filled with admiration and respect, proud of their King, Hades. King of the dead and the underworld, but also ruler of Pluto in the sign of Scorpio.

In this imaginary scene, the most important people were in front and the least behind, I was simply reproducing what I imagined the life of a king or a powerful person to be like, yet I was in an imaginary world.

An elderly believing woman came into the church and saw me completely possessed, asking her to join me on the altar, she had the reaction of making the sign of the cross and left. After this circus, I left and went to Tonio's house, where he put me up and made me sleep on a bed on his mezzanine. It was the first time I'd managed to fall asleep during a crisis, probably because I'd been working so hard.

My father came to pick me up the next morning, the sleep hadn't brought me down at all and he drove me to the hospital; that was it. I was back in psychiatry again. This time, at the hospital, I met Laura, a beautiful blonde Polish believer, very much in love, with whom I spent my days kissing. Since my release, however, I haven't seen her again, which is a shame.

I was still crazy, but she believed in me and thought I was God, even though I was getting seriously tired of it all and in my delirium. I was beginning to lose faith in myself and my dreams. It was a horrible, brutal moment of descent, and I began to suffer enormously.

I felt very bad...

Chapter 5
The depressive crisis

I was very unhappy, very unhappy, I was coming down from my deluded happiness and I was taking all the wrath of the people around me in my head, which didn't help me at all. I began to sink into depression, and all the looks I got were ones of blame: from the clever grandson. I had become the weed, the bad guy, the beast, the clown, I couldn't stand it, on top of the fact that I wasn't doing anything.

I'd stay with my grandparents and play the console sometimes with my brother Elie, I'd have to take sleeping pills to fall asleep at night, so I'd have the box with me, then I'd think so much, I couldn't feel good. It was like a huge physical pain all over my body, filled with regret, anger, low self-esteem. I was angry at myself for having been so ridiculous, and I wanted to get it over with. Less than a week after being discharged from psychiatry, I swallowed a box of sleeping pills; I really thought it would kill me but no it didn't. I woke up four days later in hospital with IVs all around me. It was a nightmare, it made me feel even worse. All I wanted to do now was die, and I couldn't do that. I asked for a disposable razor to shave with. I used it on my arms, but it hardly cut at all, so I gave up.

The nurses noticed it some time later and got worried, giving me more and more medication. There was one nurse, gentle and kind, in her forties, who tried to reason with me, but it did nothing for me. I spent whole days torturing myself, the worst suffering I'd ever felt in my life: mental suffering. I was in my hospital bed, suffering so much that I mutilated my face with my fingernails until it bled. I was suffering so much that nothing else could hurt me, I wanted to die rather than suffer so much, so deep was the pain.

After this depressive crisis, I became more or less normal again, still suffering, but better, especially after my father and grandmother understood that I was suffering from an illness and showed me their support. I was no longer blamed, I was seen as a sick person and no longer as a mental defective. This simple action on their part had partly cured me, I had regained a part of my peace, so I could leave psychiatry once again...

Chapter 6
The dictatorial crisis

Now that I've been discharged from psychiatry, it's high time I went back to school. It's 2015, and thanks to my eternal goodwill, I've enrolled in a DUT (university technology diploma) GEII (electrical engineering and industrial computing) course. I was going to resume my studies in September, and I no longer smoke, at least partially. I've also stopped taking my medication. Once again, I'm under the mistaken impression that I don't need them.

Back to school day is early September 2015, as usual, I mask my heavy past, I'm a few years older than the others.

The studies go well, the 1$\square^r$ semester in the bag, I even finish in the European group, comprising the best of the promotion. Things are going well, but at the start of the second semester, I start smoking again, replacing cigarettes with weed. I started not sleeping again.

Every day, I'd go to classes, eat at fast-food restaurants with friends and, every time, I'd end up throwing up everything I ate into the toilet. My body refused to eat; I saw it as a divine message. I'd find playing cards on the floor and associate them with messages. I'd seen one at the entrance to the village house in Carnoules before my first attack, a Queen of Spades. Anyway, I kept seeing cards alone on the ground along the way and looking up their symbolic definition on the internet.

I've always been open-minded and attracted to the esoteric. One day, I didn't want to go on, I was fed up with classes, convinced that I had a greater destiny than the one I was being offered. So, in class, I took out my cell phone several times to get myself expelled. Which I did. I then went back to my flat (my father's) on the 13□ floor in the Pontcarral housing estate in Toulon. I locked myself in my room and while smoking, I started writing again on social networks everything that crossed my mind. And here again, I hadn't been sleeping or eating for three nights already.

One evening, my father came home, smelled the grass and started to get really angry; he didn't want me to leave. He didn't want me to leave, so to make him go away, I raised my arm as if to hit him, but it was just to scare him. He got scared and went for a knife to scare me even more and calm me down. I fled, ran up the stairs to the 13□ floor. I also went to hide in the stairwells of 7□ waiting for him to give up his search. Once I thought the way was safe, I set off into the city of Toulon.

I had my credit card and my cell phone. It was dark and I saw a man on a street who looked lost. Caught up in my delirium, I spoke to him in a loud tone, asked him what he was doing there, and he told me that his wife had had a fit and broken everything in their house. I withdrew 100 euros in two bills of 50 and gave him one, adding to find me some drugs if he wanted the other bill.
He did, and then we became colleagues. He believed in my delusions, he thought I was ALLAH.

He took me to his house, showed me the damage his wife had done, and I told him all about myself and my mission. I wore a black jacket and convinced him I was the world's cop. He was as if impassioned by what I was telling him, he really thought I was the word of ALLA, of ALLAH. Understand that in this state, I believe so strongly in what I'm saying that it's difficult for someone who doesn't have all his convictions already pre-constructed not to believe me.

I walked through the city by his side as if he were my prophet, and at a crosswalk he refused to follow me. Just then, a police car arrived and took him away, with the cops telling me not to stay outside; it was crazy and made me even more convinced of my delusion. I was all-powerful and protected by the universe.

I went into the city center and came across some homeless youngsters who had seen how weak I was and wanted to take advantage of the situation by asking me if I wanted 300 euros worth of cannabis resin. I said yes, so we went to the cash dispenser, put in my credit card and entered the code. I also entered the amount of 300 euros on the screen, and the machine refused the transaction. I told the two homeless men that it was impossible and saw the girl trying again with my card. I knew she had bad intentions, so I insulted her in front of her boyfriend with words that were horrible to hear. I was the dictator. I yelled at the poor hussy, her boyfriend came up from behind, knocked me down and hit me in the face. I didn't feel a thing, and even laughed, as he went to pick up an empty beer bottle from the floor, intending to smash it over my skull. So I ran away.

I was still delirious and happy to have given them such false hope of a failed scam, my eye was blown out and I could only see out of one eye. I flagged down the first car that took me to the police station, who in turn called the fire department and said, "You see. We told you to go home". I waited for the fire department, who arrived with their truck and took me straight to Toulon's Sainte-Musse hospital.

They told me that the doctors had gone home and that I had to wait until the next day. I was delirious with him, telling him I was going to blow up Israel by sending an army, because I was Jesus and Judah had betrayed me. The security guard told me to stay calm and sit down, which I did, and then I fell asleep on the seats in the waiting room.

The next day, I went to see the doctor about my eye, but there was a queue and I was told to wait. I got fed up and left.

I left and went to the housing estate nearby. I asked some dealers if they could let me smoke for free. They said no, so I walked away from them and my jacket. I pretended to pull out a gun; they started running, which of course increased my delirium.

Afterwards, some people were looking for me, but while hiding, I set off on foot for the university. Everyone had classes at that hour, and I saw the head of the department, and the teachers, who were stunned to see me in such a state with my eye blown out. I was delirious with my teachers, whether I was talking nonsense or not, I can't remember; in any case, we had long discussions. They took me to the deputy's office, where I wanted to talk to him alone. So I aggressively ordered everyone to get out of there, which they did, and I spoke with the head of department. Then the nurse arrived, they contacted the fire department and I ended up once again at Sainte-Musse hospital.

The emergency room was overcrowded and no one was taking care of me. So I set off back to the university by bus this time; when I arrived, they were all astonished to see me again, called the fire department back and told them that this time they had to take care of me first. So I went back to the hospital, and this time the emergency staff put me in a room on a bed strapped to all four limbs as usual. They left me conscious, so I started screaming. Sometimes in those moments, I'd manage to detach an arm or a leg, but I could never get away, so I'd yell until a nurse came an hour or two later to inject me with the dose that would send me off to the psychiatric ward.

I woke up perfused as usual, but this time the doctors wanted to treat me for good. I was locked up for five months, they wanted to make sure I came down well and really, they wanted to save me. After four months, I was exhausted, fed up and starting to come down. However, they made me wait another month before discharging me and I was discharged in August 2016.

I then went on a road-trip to Spain with my father and my two brothers, Elie and Maxime. We made it all the way down to Cadiz and Gibraltar, and I decided never to touch drugs again. So I never smoked pot again from that moment on, which I did. I was 22.

Chapter 7
The Egyptian crisis

I gave up the idea of continuing my DUT GEII. For a year, from 2016 to 2017, I had nothing left to do, I had to keep busy, so I found a civic service mission that involved accompanying patients in the context of hospitalization. It involved looking after patients with multiple disabilities. I had a job interview, and there were about seven applicants. I did my interview with the director of the establishment by videoconference and explained my motivations. They seemed satisfied and I was right.

Some time later, I was hired for a seven-month assignment, which I successfully completed, and everyone was satisfied with me. I took a month's leave from my civic contract to do a two-month summer season in Savoie as a surface technician and dishwasher in a vacation village in Lanslevillard. It's a ski resort perched at an average altitude of 2,500 meters in the Haute Maurienne, with a population of five hundred. Maurienne, home of the famous cutler Joseph Opinel.

I stayed there for the whole summer. It was so cool that I decided to stop taking my pills, so as not to feel under the constraints of my illness. I told my grandmother that since I no longer smoked, stopping the pills wouldn't be a problem. I was convinced that it was only the cannabis that was the least of my worries. My season was coming to an end that already in September 2017, I was due to enter a BTS (brevet de technicien supérieur) in computer science and digital science at the Lycée Thomas Edison in Lorgues. I wasn't delirious at all and I was proud of myself, proud that I'd been able to work for eight months without a crisis and proud to be going back to school. So I was in boarding school and most of my term went perfectly, I always got the best marks; it was cool.

During the All Saints' vacation, I went back to my grandparents' and started writing on the Internet as I used to do. I did it until I lost sleep, lost my appetite and started to rave again, in increments. I was Osiris, or rather all the Egyptian gods. On my birthday, my grandparents invited me to eat in the Salle Honoré Daumier in Carnoules. I left before the end, all excited, and crashed my car into a concrete block. The whole passenger side was in ruins and I'd hit my head hard against the steering wheel, cracking my eyebrow.

These events sent me back into delirium, as if given the chaos I'd created, I had to find a solution, and the solution was to flee, to plunge into my dreams, which I did. My father found me and when he saw me, he immediately called the fire department who took me to the emergency room. My father was with me at the hospital and when I arrived, I saw a nurse at reception playing with his cell phone. I went up to him and smashed the computer on the reception desk with my fist, shouting "Bosse, you rat! I was mad. After that, they tied me to a bed, and I flirted with the nurses, convinced that I was Osiris.

I could see hieroglyphics in every blood results paper, my brain was firing on all cylinders and dreams were intertwined with reality. Anyway, after this episode, I ended up for the 6□ time in a psychiatric internship. During this stay, I met the second great love of my life: Rachel, a Hyéroise girl three years younger than me, a very beautiful blonde with brown eyes and a really intelligent girl. She was very feminine and seemed so fragile; she had everything to please me. When I saw her, I immediately fell madly in love. Even though she was a bit paranoid and heard voices, she was so sweet and kind. Then I caught her eye and took her by the hips to Palmiers 2, a different ward from the one I usually go to (the Odyssey) at Pierrefeu hospital (Henri Guérin).

When I got out in February 2018, we became a couple and for seven months I lived love with her in my father's apartment in Pontcarral. So I lived happily ever after with her there, and I'll always have wonderful memories of our story.

Chapter 8
The Unraveling : Endgame 1

Once out of hospital, as previously stated, I lived with Rachel in my apartment (well, my father's apartment) in Toulon, and I was careful to take all my pills every night.

I loved Rachel and I wanted her to pull through, I got her to stop taking drugs, even cigarettes, I wanted to take the opportunity, while we were recovering, to talk about the future and I advised her to go back to school and pass her A-levels. I took her to all her appointments, I had taken on the role of father that she hadn't had, but it didn't bother me that much in the end, I did everything for her, right up until the start of the new school year.

I had enrolled in GEA (Gestion d'entreprise et d'administration) at La Garde, another course also preparing for a DUT. She enrolled to take her baccalaureate at the Lycée Bonaparte in Toulon, which is right next to the Alexandre 1□ʳ garden (another sign likely to stroke my delusion in the direction of the hair). One day, at the start of the school year, as I was walking back to the flat, I caught the smell of grass. I'd figured out that she smoked, so I was furious, because I was planning a bright future and she was throwing it all away to enjoy, as they all say, youth.

We split up, and today I've passed my GEA semester with flying colors, and the lithium I've been ingesting has kept me in a decent state for over a year now, a record for me. Even if my separation from Rachel has certainly destroyed me. In fact, I think the fact that I'm in low spirits contributes to my success at school, because it's harder to get off the ground when you're feeling down.

Nevertheless, I have the strong feeling that I was a great fool to have listened to the doctors so late, but now I do. They've stabilized me wonderfully, my brain isn't racing any more, although I still have great highs and lows, but they're not pushed to extremes. Unfortunately, suffering, the breach that affects us all to a greater or lesser extent, cannot be healed, or I would no longer be vulnerable to the mood swings I suffer from.

Chapter 9
The conquest of power

Now my second semester is under way, morale is rising again, I'm passing without too much difficulty, I love studying and I love this course. Alongside my courses, I meet a lot of girls, some of whom I plan to date in the future, but it all falls through because my expectations are different from theirs, and they're not the right ones.

At the end of the semester, I am ranked 7□ in this class of around a hundred students, I complete my internship in an accounting firm and everything is still going wonderfully. My supervisor is really satisfied and even tells me about the opportunities he has to offer me for my future. Absolutely, everything's perfect, but at the end of the internship, I suddenly found myself without work for the 2019 summer vacations, and there it was, an open door to the freedom of thought, intellectual ardor and imagination that have always driven me.

I gradually began to cultivate my extraordinary ideas and my "divine" megalomania.

During the last week of the vacations, I decided to reduce my medication intake to once every two days, since I thought I could do so without any consequences. My thoughts of being persecuted by pills had resurfaced. I wanted to be happy, full of life, I wanted to unleash the beast, and I did. I had a breakdown, as I say now.

I started my second year of GEA at the beginning of September, and on my first day of college, I went in completely psycho. I attended classes with a good attendance record, but my mind was entirely elsewhere. It had taken refuge in the world of dreams, in music titled with my first name, in particular one entitled "Alexandre's Dream" by the group Smok, which bears the same name and has the same typography as the brand of electronic cigarettes I vapotage.

As I've always smoked Lucky Strike cigarettes, I also listened to Juliette Armanet's song "Alexandre" over and over again, where, and I quote: "Alexandre, I'd give my whole life for an ash, just an ash, of your Lucky...". I made the connection with my father's nickname (Lucky).

In my spare time, I'd take a selfie in the University of La Garde, with the university buildings in the background. Building A for Alexandre, Building B for Bertorello and the EVE building, this one for my Goddess (music for this very moment: Asking Alexandria, "EVE").

In short, I was on Noah's boat. On the way back to my grandparents', same melody, loss of sleep, loss of appetite. I got into a tangle with my father, who called the fire department. When they arrived, I knew for the first time how to bring down my internal pressure, I turned into a fine manipulative strategist; I didn't want my father to be right about my psychotic happiness. The fire department saw me as a good guy, or at least I worked for it, and it worked. They did, however, offer to put me in hospital for observation, which I accepted.

I let my ardor take a back seat during the one-night stay until the next day's consultation with the psychiatrist, who deemed me perfectly suitable and discharged me. My plan had gone exactly according to plan. So I left the emergency room and set off walking from the hospital in Hyères to the Sauvebonne valley, about 15 kilometers, hitchhiking barefoot (my shoes were too small), and a friendly motorist took me to the village of Pierrefeu.

From there, I went to the police station. The chief of the Pierrefeu Gendarmerie Brigade, whom I sincerely appreciate, accompanied me with other gendarmes to help me get my things back, and thus avoid any trouble with my father. Once again, I was in complete control of my decompensation, so much so that they couldn't notice the state I was really in. I camouflaged my crisis as if it were a matter of life and death. Freedom or hospitalization...

Once I'd packed the essentials into my room at my grandparents', I jumped in my car and my interstellar road-trip could begin. I drove to La Capte, in Hyères, where Rachel lives, hoping to see her again. As I arrived, I saw a car pull up in front of me with the front passenger and the driver getting out of the car. Both opened the rear door and beat the rear passenger out of the car. They saw me and ran off. The victim of this cinema, quite naturally, stood up in the driver's seat and drove off in what looked like his car. Anyway, it was crazy.

At the time, for me, it was normal. Yes, the advent of my New World Order had to happen this way, with violence and a lot of disregard for all pre-established rules, it had to start with a breakthrough of anarchy.

I didn't see Rachel, but I stretched out on the beach and took a selfie in the evening. I returned to Carnoules, ordered a pizza and a bottle of soda, which I consumed in the village church, willingly asking permission from the priest who, despite his displeasure, agreed. I devoured my pizza while talking to a parishioner. I tried to persuade him that the one on the cross with the nails was me. I asked him to call the Vatican so I could meet the Pope. He had no faith in me, the vulnerable, poor sinner.

So I finished my pizza, and spent the night sleeping in my car at Notre-Dame-des-Anges, hoping to rediscover the bond I'd had, five years earlier, with the beautiful and longed-for Camille. That link that haunts me every time I see the Crédit Agricole logo, the C that embraces the A, every time we talk about cami(lle)sole or kami(camille)kaze...

I slept well, even too well, a good night. As soon as I woke up, I was off again, driving to Toulon, squatting on the benches, chatting with the seagulls, trying to tame them. At one point, I saw a tethered dog barking and showing its teeth, next to its owner, who told me to watch out for it. Without listening to him, I went over to the fearless dog, stroked him hard and untied him, telling his master to let him go free, otherwise he'd goat him.

Then I went to Faron Zoo. I wanted to get into the cage with them, tame them and walk around town with them, the normal thing for a psycho. The guards wouldn't let me, so I looked at the lions in the presence of the guards and told them to eat them as soon as they got the chance. Afterwards, I found myself annoying the chimpanzees through the fence, trying to get them to revolt by showing them what he had to do to ruin the fence. At one point, one even did what I did, shaking the fence and pretending to want to get out. I had the impression that he'd understood what I was trying to convey to him. I was happy, I'd got the message across and I left.

I got back in the car and had an epiphany. I thought back to the time when my friend Fred, a good friend from high school, blond and with many years of boxing under his belt, and I went to look at the Fort de Brégançon from the surrounding hills. Then it hit me: we were heading for the vacation home of our President of the Republic.

I park my car in front of the first gate. I leave it, take a selfie next to the gate and then drive on, jumping it. I gradually make my way onto the property, taking selfies to show my network "friends" my progress. I climb the second gate and arrive on the island, where the sea was raging. I reached the fort's large gate and shouted "Macron! The guard arrived, astonished to see me in front of the gate of this little fortress, and with the fear I could see in his eyes, he said to me: "He's not here, what do you want? I told him I was Osiris, that I wanted to see Macron to discuss politics and the establishment of my New World Order. He told me to leave, I insulted him, his wife arrived and started getting angry with me.

A reaction, a mistake, unfortunately for her, I insulted her and her boyfriend quite brutally. I told them I was going to climb up and make a mess. They believed me and left for the even more protected presidential part of the fort. I climbed the gate like an assassin (reference: Assassin's Creed, the game for connoisseurs). I entered the first part of the fort, was inside and made my way to the front door of the presidential residence. I poured out my rage on everything I could find, smashing flowerpots and throwing them to the ground. I kicked the janitor's Kangoo to pieces, twisting the windscreen wipers and pulverizing the rear-view mirrors. Then I went back down to the guard's dressing room, kicked in the glass door and, as I entered his dressing room, took a selfie. I took a selfie.

It was my home from then on, and shortly afterwards I went outside to take a photo. I then saw three gendarmes armed with guns in a state of emergency, while I flitted about with my camera. They handcuffed me and took me to the gendarmerie. I was held in custody for thirty minutes, while they made their transcriptions, even mentioning my demands to the Head of State. Which were still my demands for the establishment of my New

World Order. I wonder if this story ever reached the ears of the head of the armed forces, although it really doesn't matter to me. A psychiatrist came to see me and asked how I was, to which I replied "very well, especially since the angels are my friends and I dominate and subdue the demons". He told me he'd understood, he'd basically understood that I needed to be hospitalized. So here I am, back at the Pierrefeu hospital.

Chapter 10
The brief resumption of
a normal existence

On arrival at Palmiers 1, the nurses laughed to see me again, or rather to know what I'd done. As usual, they brought me down a peg or two.

To end my involuntary hospitalization, once the beast in me had become docile again, they put me in a freer pavilion, as usual, the Odyssée. I met this girl, whom I nicknamed Lo, after her first name Loreleï, a dark-haired brunette, also very beautiful, a year younger than me and originally from Toulouse, on vacation in Hyères with her cousin. She had decompensated like me. The first time I saw her, she was completely turned on, so I went over to her and we exchanged our first kiss, which she never remembered. Unfortunately, she was too far out in space at the time.

So much so that that very evening, they had transferred her to the intensive pavilion I'd just landed in, Les Palmiers 1. A few days later, I saw her, looked at her with a piercing, unvarnished gaze and took her under my wing. She was calmer, came back down, we sat on a bench and kissed, it was magnificent. She became my darling, my princess. I didn't see her for long at first, until she came back to the Odyssey. We exchanged a lot, I understood her, we created a very strong bond. So strong that shortly after its release in early 2020, we flew to Madrid, Spain, as lovers. So in love that afterwards, she came to live with me at my grandparents'. This came in handy for the first containment of the 2020 Covid-19 pandemic.

We were creative, cultivating my grandfather's land, creating a small vegetable garden. We took care of the house, we were active, too active even. Especially since I'd asked my shrink to take me off neuroleptics to try to be stable without taking them, and above all because of the side effects. This proved fatal for me...

Chapter 11
The French Revolution and the capture of Versailles

When I stopped taking the neuroleptics, I became irritable and couldn't tolerate the slightest remark. I was a perfectionist, trying to do things right, and I'd lose my temper at the slightest criticism; I'd entered a hypomanic phase. My body was exhausted, and my mind was ordering me to continue my efforts, which led to major conflicts with my grandparents, who stimulated me even more.

At one point, it was one conflict too many with my grandmother, who is often worried and on my back. I got Lo into the car and off we went. We stood on the sand at the beach in La Capte, it was the end of May 2020, the weather was good, we were fine, but my father arrived and called the fire department. It was lost forever, one stimulation too many that made me take off without my shoes with Lo.

While we waited for the fire department to leave, we hid in the car and made our way to the starting point of the revolution, Marseille.

Arriving in the city by car, I took the streetcar lanes to the old port and then found myself on a bus lane. When they got close enough, and I didn't feel like talking to them, I stepped on the gas pedal in what they call "refus d'obtempérer". The national police motorcyclists came after me and signalled for me to stop, which I did, even though their guns were pointed at me.

That time, there was a team of reporters from the program "Au cœur de l'enquête" on the subject of brawls and chases in Marseille, who interviewed me and put my exploit on TV. That was pretty funny too. Then the police took me to the station, asked me questions and noticed that I was calm. They called my psychiatrist and eventually released me. I met up with my princess, Lo, who was waiting for me at reception. We went to the impound lot to pick up the car, but a paper from the police station was missing. We backed up and went back, but there were a lot of people waiting for their turn out front. As luck would have it, there was a Black Lives Matter demonstration. So the cops closed the police station reception and everyone dispersed.

I, in my madness, had targeted the demonstrators; once they were in front of the police station. I flipped them off and made all sorts of despicable gestures, Lo too. It was my entertainment to provoke three hundred people, some of whom wanted to form groups against me, and I went straight for them. They didn't dare touch me, because I was devoid of all fear and I think I was instilling in them the fear I didn't have. They decided to continue the march. A cop, in awe of my provocation, asked for my first name, my surname and Lo's, then gave us priority, to collect the paper for the car. Mission accomplished, now it was on to the next stage...

Lo and I picked up the car, which had an electronic toll tag. We put the GPS in the German car I had (well, a grey Volkswagen Polo), heading for Versailles on the A7. On the freeway, there was a lane marked with orange bollards for overtaking cars. I hit one of them at full speed and it partially detached the bumper.

We arrived in Versailles in the 78 department (reminding me of Notre Dame Des Anges' altitude of 780 meters) of eighty-five thousand inhabitants, with the bumper scraping the ground and making a deafening noise. Imagine arriving in the King's city with a car that made a loud "Grrr"! It didn't take long for the police to impound it. As I'd arrived at my destination, I didn't want my car any more, I wanted to give it to the pound and have no more problems of that kind. So I gave it up.

So that was it, I was there, I was at Versailles. My château was there in front of me...

Later, as Lo and I moped around, we passed by not only the Château, but also the Saint-Louis Cathedral in Versailles, and I became delirious. We were going to do our rituals there, in my house, the house of God. Lo and I entered the cathedral and we commandeered the altar's holy place. From there, I invited her to sit on what I call the golden throne of the altar. She did so, then the first parishioner forbade me to stay, so I said to her in a devilish voice, "You get the hell out of my house!" She got scared and went off to pray, with me calmly following. She got down on her knees and prayed facing Christ. As I passed behind her, during her prayers, I told her to carry on, that it was all very well, and then I joined Lo behind the altar, facing the audience of tourists and visitors.
Another parishioner came to forbid me once again to be where I was. I had the same retort as for the first, in the same tone, but she, instead of going to pray, went to denounce me to her colleague.

I followed her to the administrative rooms with a slow but diabolical step, she started to run and, screaming, took refuge in a room through its semi-glazed door. I had no intention of hurting her, I just wanted to traumatize her so she'd leave us alone. So I punched the glass door with my right arm, which was cut open at the level of the biceps brachii, itself cut in two. I withdrew my arm and, seeing the result, the first idea that came to me was to paint the cathedral with my blood.

So I went to the altar covered with a white sheet, pumping the blood out of my wound with my right hand. I then drew a red circle of my blood around the altar, on this famous sheet. Finally, on what I call the curved marble throne to the right of the golden throne, I positioned my arm so that my blood trickled from this marbled seat to the floor, then I lay down on the parterre and the firemen arrived.

On arrival at the hospital, I was guarded by a rotation of two policemen, until the nurses shot me and then operated on my arm. My first memory was twenty-one days later, the day they took me out of my isolation room at the Charcot hospital in Plaisir. The twenty-one days leading up to that moment are not part of my memory.

When I got out, I noticed that my isolation room was at the top of a staircase that read "Staircase to Isis", which is none other than Osiris' wife in Egyptian mythology. Once again, this reinforced my delusion.

Chapter 12
Conclusion : Endgame 2

I was released from isolation at the psychiatric hospital in Plaisir, a town of thirty-thousand inhabitants also in the 78 region, not far from Versailles. I was really dosed up on meds; because of the Valium[8] , I couldn't even read the text on my cell phone. The car wasn't so bad, but unfortunately for Lo and me, this episode was the end of our story, since they wouldn't let us see each other and she was angry with me because when I'm in crisis, I can be really bad. It still destroys me today to have been with her.

All that anger and the energy that emanates from it, which is buried inside me, will always surprise me, as I am by nature calm, gentle, fairly reserved and generally introverted. I'd like to believe that this wound will one day heal, but frankly, I have little hope of that happening.

Nevertheless, in order to pursue my goals, I must exorcise myself from this anger, but if I haven't found the solution, I must learn to live with it. I know that this rift will be inside me for a long time to come, ready to open up and let out the darkness that has built up over time in the depths of my guts.

Today, I'm 26 years old, and since I was discharged at the end of 2020, the medical profession has understood that it was more than necessary for me to have a more in-depth follow-up.

---

[8] Valium: a benzodiazepine with anxiolytic, sedative, amnesic and hypnotic properties.

I practise mindfulness meditation in groups, which leads to letting go and accepting events simply as they are. Without constantly seeking to control them, we can't inevitably act for the future or the past. Thanks to these sessions, we learn to be present in the moment, to desert the mental sphere and develop the beginner's mind we all went through as children: that wonder at everything, even the most trivial or unpleasant.

With Céline, my nurse at the medical-psychological center, I'm also doing a lot of psychotherapy, which is really helping me to put words to what ails me, to defuse this bomb inside me. I've also learnt communication techniques to quell conflict, in particular how to stop using an accusatory tone of voice when dealing with someone you're angry with. It's a very rewarding way of gaining the tools to achieve a certain wisdom.

I also take part in sessions of interpersonal therapy with adjustment of social rhythms (TIPARS). These are discussion groups in which we share our experiences and relate them to the theory conveyed to us by our carers. This helps me to do a great deal of introspection, and to understand, as best I can, the origins of my manic phases.

In short, I won't try to play with the meds any more, because even if they only space out the crises, they form a real barrier, even if it's only a third of the way effective, to decompensation. I'm keeping my fingers crossed, hoping that these phases of furious madness will cease, especially if I want to complete my projects...

Apart from all that, I'm happy with nothing, I'm amazed by everything, even the unpleasant. I've learned a great deal from these experiences, even if they may seem pointless to you. For me, it's quite the opposite: thanks to them, I've been able to see what's deep inside me, my true face, stripped of all social masks. I was able to learn the notion of freedom, yes, the freedom that belongs to us when we break free from societal inhibitions.

Finding the freedom to be who we really are in front of others, without any mental barriers of our own preventing us from doing so, I find that there's nothing more enriching.

I touched my dreams - mine, not those coveted by the majority. I've grasped Albert Camus' theory of the absurd, yes, I have, and in my delirium I've entertained the idea that I have eternal life at my disposal.

I've been to hell several times, and I always come out unscathed, which forges in me an iron personality and identity. I've really hardened myself, and thanks to that I know that even if the worst were to happen to me . I'd come out of it forever and, each time, bigger and bigger! (Like Alexander, not me but the emperor).

The list is too long to enumerate all the lessons I've learned from these events, from outbursts and decompensation, but most of you will only remember the dark, gloomy and worrying picture of a person with bipolar disorder, in crisis.

I sincerely hope that this book will give you a different view of this disorder, which for many of you remains taboo. It's important that "sufferers" should speak out, that they should be proud to have this vulnerability, which is conducive to creativity and activities of all kinds. This fragility allows us to transcend our own human limits.

It's a godsend for us to have this energy, a real sense of enlightenment and, at the same time, a sacrifice of our normal, gaping existence.   Every decompensation is an unhooking, a simple unhooking from everything around us. The hospital allows us to return to the mainstream. We're really lucky to have such facilities.

Above all, remember to open up with a touch of naivety to the world in which you live, without making wild deliberations devoid of all knowledge and history of any subject whatsoever.

The simple fact of behaving in this way will open your eyes and allow you to find real treasures where you least expected it, while earning stars in your eyes for a long time to come.

Chapter 13
The Apocalyptic Crisis

Here we are in 2021, COVID-19 restrictions are easing, cannabidiol[9] or CBD for those in the know, is becoming legal, and stores selling the stuff are springing up all over France. I've been doing a lot of research on the subject, and the information I've gathered suggests that it's a good thing for people suffering from type 1 bipolar disorder, as it can even considerably reduce their attacks.

So, all in excess, I start smoking it, hoping it will have a positive effect on me. For psychiatry, it's quite the opposite, for them CBD has a negative effect, but at this point, I tell myself to let them interpret what they want in the same way that I have the right to interpret what I want. I'm planning to enroll in medicine at the Faculty of Nice, but with the PASS reform (formerly PACES) and LAS (health access license), I no longer have the right to repeat a year in PASS and I have to opt for a health access license on parcours sup.

So I chose a degree that suited me best, i.e. the MIASHS degree (degree in mathematics and computer science applied to the humanities), but of course, with my chaotic student history as the selection results approached, I was very poorly ranked for the health course, so I applied for the degree alone without health access, which I was accepted into.

Looking forward to September, the start of the new school year, I'm looking for a studio to live in for my studies, and I've found a 17 m² apartment in La Trinité,

---

[9] Cannabidiol: cannabinoid found in cannabis

near Nice, in an ideal location for a student like me. So I'm rushing to become the tenant and sign the lease.

While I'm waiting for the new school year to start, I spend my time looking after my budgies, working on this book and in the summer I got a baby magpie back from a nest that I nicknamed Persephone, whom I'm taming and who fills me with the only true friendship there could be, that between an animal and its "master".

My game had resumed its course, so I was off to the Trinity, which in Christianity represents the one God, the Father, the Son and the Holy Spirit. In short, it was back to a shoot of mythology or theology, call it what you will! All my beliefs were back in action, but this time it was serious, I was finally opening my eyes once and for all to everything around me: for some spiritual people, my third eye or pineal gland had opened, I was enlightened.

All the words containing AL represented Alexander's prefix AL and Bertorello's prefix, "Bert". When combined, this gave ALBERT, like Prince Albert, or Albert Einstein, pioneer of the theory of general relativity (ALExandre), Camus pioneer of the theory of the ABsurde (with AB, the initials of my first and last names) or Albert Pike, who for thirty-two years headed one of the most important components of Freemasonry in the United States: the Supreme Council of the Southern Jurisdiction of the Ancient and Accepted Scottish Rite.

By the way, Freemasonry's 300th anniversary took place in 2017 at the RoyAL ALBERT Hall in London. The Masonic symbols represented my name, my NOM (my New World Order). The compass for A, the square for L and the G. In short, it's ALG, Alexander The Great, but I prefer to say Alexander The Giant, since the great one died in battle.

What's more, I come from a family of true Masons (without the Franc word). Also, I like to think that my grandfather is the best mason on the planet, given all he knows how to do and the empire he built.

Then I got fixated on my date of birth, October 29 (10) 1994, and when people ask "What's new?", I realized they were saying "What's 2 9? After that, the number 10 (October) in soccer was worn by some of the greatest players in the history of the game.

Finally, let's deal with the most important, 94: when we add 9+4, we get 13, which is the greatest number of death from 0 and 100 (scorpion, Hades the god of the dead[10]) as the number from 0 to 100 representing the number of the "reaper", thus 13.

---

[10] See chapter 4

MARSeille (Mars is a planet that rules the sign of Scorpio with Pluto), its department number (Bouches-du-Rhône) is 13, then there are 49, 58, 67, 76, 85 and 94, I'll let you do the math. Finally, the Var (83) landline telephone number starts with **0494**, always a plus sign.

Coming back to the ALLAH religion in Arabic الله, I see a snake from Christian Genesis with a scythe, the scythe of the reaper. Finally, I have a pretty good relationship with death compared to most people, the dead push me and make my strength and as they don't come back it's because most of them are well where they are.

When I opened my eyes, I became the Great Architect of the Universe, the GADLU. For those in the know, the great all-seeing eye, which isn't a mistake, since I observe everything and especially all the creations of others.

In films such as "Scarface", the man who kills the film's main character Tony Montana, played by AL Paccino, is a powerful mafioso with the bizarre name of Alejandro Sosa.

In "Into the Wild", 22-year-old Christopher McCandless, a brilliant student, leaves everything behind to live self-sufficiently in the forest and earns the nickname "Alexander Super Tramp". I'm not going to list all the films, characters, music and raps that I refer to in my ramblings, but I'll let you do your own research if you're interested in the Scorpio emperor ascending Virgin Mary that I am. If you prefer, I have total control over the world as a whole. I'm also the little product of the multinationals who've come to put order on Earth, of course through Chaos. Ordo Ab Chaos (Order born of Chaos).

Shall we continue? I'm like orAL-B, all-in-one, I'm Horus, son of my father Osiris and my mother Isis. My right eye represents the sun, my left eye the moon and my body the universe. In short, I'm the one God of the monotheists and the God of gods of the polytheists. At least that's clear, and my aim isn't to stay on this little blue planet, which is far too small for my liking.

In short, I continued to write and thus to spread my psychological power over the world all summer long with Perseus (Persephone) without sleeping for nights on end, totally sleepless, I put my music on my speaker, I had reattained enlightenment, and so my aggressiveness had returned in full force.

My grandfather, with his white hair and green eyes like mine, who likes to have control over his environment - in short, a scorpion thing - had ordered me to turn down the music on my speaker. Unfortunately, you don't give orders to a madman if you don't want him to become offended and aggressive, always verbally speaking of course. So I insulted my grandparents, which of course I'll always regret, as I do when it happens to my father. However, for me it was to dominate, it was for a holy and just cause fraternity, equality and finally freedom and not freedom first.

The next day, they called the fire department, who came to collect me and take me to the hospital in Hyères, which I now know very well. Talking to some young people, I waited for an appointment with a psychiatrist who never arrived. I then consulted a nurse who found me completely adapted to life in society. She then let me go and my grandfather, who had now understood my pathology or theology (as far as I was concerned) and who didn't hold it against me, came to pick me up in the middle of town, at last at the Hyères media library near the casino.

In the car, I told him a lot about my plan and whatever I told him about myself, he drank it down like holy water. Then I went back to their place and the Hollywood had started again. I got mixed up with them again, but "thanks" to my uncle Lionel, deputy mayor of Carnoules, dark-haired with black eyes, ten years younger than his brother, my father, when the gendarmerie arrived. He told them I was having major delirious flashes, so I ended up in Pierrefeu once again, at Les Palmiers 1, then quickly at L'Odyssée.

I realized that I was "Simba" from Disney's "The Lion King", my father "Mouffassa" was born on August 18, 1969 with the zodiac sign lion, 69 in his year of birth, like the department of Lyon, and my uncle was born 10 years later on August 5, 1979 with the zodiac sign lion too, so I'll let you guess who he represents "Scar" even if he remains my favorite uncle. Especially since he did almost all my schoolwork.

In psychiatry, at the Odyssey, in the midst of enlightenment, I met Marine, my magnificent goddess of the sign Pisces, my beautiful mermaid who meets the beast, in this case me, in the abyss (the Odyssey). I invite you to listen to "Marine" by Claire Gimatt, a song I was raving about with her. To tell the truth, Marine melts me with her eyes, her beauty, her intelligence and especially her sweetness. She's Lebanese, chestnut brown with brown eyes. This was her first hospitalization and, of course, she was terrified. So I talked to her, even though I was scaring her with my big Loxapac eyes[11] . I then put on my Ray ban and gave her my book (the 2□ edition) which she read that

[11] Loxapac: an antipsychotic, leader of the dibenzo-oxazepine family.

evening and the next day her view of me had completely changed, I think my book had opened her eyes to my pathology. Then she and I fell madly in love, so as usual I began a new love affair with her. After that, she went out and came to see me often, and then it was my turn to go out after spending my leave with her.

When I got out, I often went to her house, as it was autumn. While staying with my grandparents and keeping in touch with Marine, I remember that one night I spent my nights contemplating the sky, especially the constellation of Orion. Myriads of shooting stars streaked across the sky, and I thought they were angels coming to join me on Earth!

I told myself in my head that they didn't need to fall and that everything was already under control, that I'd already pulled off a coup d'état on the solar system.

I was left with this insignificant, blue planet called Earth.

At that very moment, I was being persecuted by the whole world and I had a duty to persecute the world, and that's what I've done throughout my manic phases to this day.

Chapter 14
The resentment of offense

December 15 was approaching and a meal was organized at my grandparents'. Everything went perfectly until my father, the lion, came looking for me, or "biting" me if you prefer; he hurt me where my wound had never closed. First, he said behind my back that he preferred my brother Elie to me. Then he called me a dirty Arab, and that's when it started to piss me off. On Facebook, I had threatened the blasphemous priests who call themselves "my father" since the holy father, the only God, is me.

With a photo of my hunting knife in hand, my father Jean-Luc hurriedly tossed it to my grandmother. I apologize to my inner peace, but I saw blood red. I grabbed my hunting knife and, like an AL Qaeda or D'Isis of the Islamic State terrorist, went after him with it. Well, let's just say it was the other side of the coin, since he'd done it to me at Pontcarral too (see previous chapters), but he called police, fireman, ambulance, in short, blue, white and red, the three colors associated with each of these professions.

As usual, I escaped and then my grandfather hid me. I loved having such a strong bond with him for the first time. I was wanted by the gendarmerie, who wanted to put my photo in the media, and then I took off with my polo shirt to my Notre-Dame-Des-Anges headquarters.

I called Marine, with whom I was separated, and she invited me to her place. The next day, we had to take her mother's cat back to the old town of Hyères, which we did, and then we ended up in a traffic jam. There was a truck delivering two or three boxes to an apartment, behind the truck was a woman in her car and behind her an angry man who was honking his horn and making obscene gestures at the woman who was trying to calm him down.

I saw blood red, got out of my Polo, smashed his rear-view mirror, opened his door, grabbed him by the collar, insulted him and got back into my car, hoping he'd "bugger off". The fat "bastard" closed all his doors and windows to call the police and just stood there. I spun around again, got out again, his rear window was ajar and with my right hand, I smashed it to smithereens and grabbed him by the collar. He was on the phone with the cops, crying and saying "come quick, I'm with a real madman, he's going to kill me!

Marine picked me up crying, calmed me down, took me back to my car and put me in reverse, which I did, and the other one did the same so I wouldn't run away. So I shifted back and he thought he'd won the game. I pulled up behind him and reversed violently. I then slammed into his rear bumper four times until he bailed, which he did. My car was dead, the engine overheated, so I left it stranded in the middle of old Hyères and we took an Uber cab to Marine's in La Garde.

She left to run some errands, the Guard police station summoned her to find out if she was in danger, which she denied. She said I was at home watching Malcolm, which is what I was doing. At the same time, she offered to send a team to pick me up for safety reasons, which she refused.

Finally, the Hyères police station contacted me and suggested I come that evening, at the risk of sleeping in police custody all night or waiting until the next morning for the transcript. I chose the second option, and at dawn I went with Marine to the comico. I spent two hours recounting the "event" without a single lie, because lying is the first sin in Genesis. It's also the most widespread sin on earth. So when you want God's clemency, you don't lie, and I hope that one day you'll understand that. Finally, I stayed in police custody until 3 p.m. waiting for the expert psychiatrist to whom I told my beliefs and judged me irresponsible, and then I ended up this time directly at the odyssey. The cops all said goodbye to me despite the fact that they were sending me to psychiatry; they had understood my values of fraternity, which were too dear to me.

I stayed there for seven months, "controlling" the world from my smartphone. I even proposed to Putin in my delirious trip to join the New World Order's global governance, which he refused, so I advanced my pawns, NATO[12] in the direction of Russia and triggered the beginnings of war in Ukraine. So, if you don't want me to blow everything up, and you along with it, stick to your guns - that's the moral of this part of my life. You can laugh with me, the BAAL (Bertorello Alexandre ALexandre), but don't overdo it.

Finally, I separated from Marine for the second time on the day of the presidential elections when I put Macron back in power and excluded the candidate Marine Lepen. Marine had taken that politician's place in my mind, and there were still a lot of insecurities between me and her linked to my crises. All I could do was talk deliriously, and I still remembered the name Camille.

I suffered from this separation with Marine, but her parents did everything to keep me away from her without knowing me, and as I was in crisis, their plan had worked.

---

[12] NATO: North Atlantic Organization (Allies)

Our relationship was on the rocks and unfortunately, when I made the choice to separate from her, I didn't think she would suffer from it. I felt I had total control over external events, but not this one.

My whole life was connected with people in high places. I was also completely out of touch with reality, so it was impossible for me to manage any relationship, even if I was in love with this Lebanese princess.

Chapter 15
The flight to conquer Rome

After seven months in psychiatry, you can understand, especially when you're 27 and have rabies. I spat on a psychiatrist who had told Marine to "stay away from Alexandre, he's incurable", noting that my favorite expression when dealing with carers was "you're sick of making me believe that I am". He threatened to put me in P1 (Palmiers 1), not knowing who he was attacking. I went after him, insulting him, the nurses surrounded him to protect him, then Hélène, "my mother at heart", a friend of my father's, took me aside and we had a frank talk. She's great, because she managed to calm me down just when I was feeling like killing myself.

Every week, I asked my classy Italian doctor for permission to visit my grandparents. I'd take my car and tour the Var in my Polo, without sleeping every night. I often went to Notre-Dame-des-Anges. At the 8☐ or 9☐ permission, on Friday, I flipped my cable, I took my car. I then sped off in the middle of the night on the freeway towards Italy, given that the ARS[13] du Var refused my transfer to Nice.

---

[13] ARS : Regional Health Agency

Arriving in Italy, I stopped to fill up with diesel on the freeway and my car wouldn't start - the choke had given up the ghost. I tried to push it on the freeway to get it to start in second gear, but I couldn't do it. So I called the emergency services, who took the car to Borghetto di Vara, a village of nine hundred and fifty inhabitants in the province of La Spezia, in the north-western region of Liguria.

As it was Saturday night, I had to wait until Monday as it was the weekend and the garage was closed. So I decided to crash in my car and do some sightseeing around this wonderfully flowery village. Once again, I felt super happy and free. I took a selfie in front of the churchyard next to my car in the middle of the night.

Then I'd be out and about 24/7, sleeping very little. In the village, I'd buy breakfasts and sit on bar terraces drinking iced tea, my favorite beverage, while smoking my tobacco, Amerindian style.

On Monday, the mechanic came and managed to start my car in second gear. He advised me to return to France to have it repaired, which of course I didn't do. So off I went to Rome, taking great care not to stall my car for four hundred and forty kilometers, while taking the national roads to discover the landscape. Frankly, Italy is magnificent, as are the people, even if there are assholes everywhere, but everyone knows that. Well, I say jerk, but for me, there's nothing more jerkish than the word itself.

When I arrived in Rome, I parked my car at Ciampino on the outskirts and took off in the direction of the metro, abandoning my car because its problems had bored me to tears. I needed a vacation and I didn't hesitate to take it: I stopped with the A line at san Petro (St. Peter's) of course, with the Vatican as my priority, then walked for hours in the heat of this year 2022. I toured the city and visited everything on foot, to the point of my feet hurting. On the other hand, this didn't stop me from moving forward; on the contrary, suffering and self-flagellation are redemptive for me.

I was completely enlightened, so I stopped at a restaurant near Saint-Pierre for some pasta bolognese. An African wanted to sell me a bracelet while I was eating, so I said, "Look, I don't have any change on me. But I do have my card, so if you want, I'll give you the code and you can have thirty euros. He said, "Come with me to do it", to which I replied, raising my voice, "Listen, I'm eating. You're not going to break my balls or you're going to take my fucking card. I'll give you the code and you can withdraw your thirty euros yourself". He said "okay" and I added "but don't give me that". I pointed my two fingers at my eyes and then at his, telling him that if he played with me, I'd find him, and then it wouldn't be the same. He listened to me and withdrew his thirty euros, then came back half an hour later and put the card where I'd ordered him to put it. He offered me a bracelet, which I reluctantly accepted as he needed it more than I did.

The restaurant I'd set up in was empty before I arrived. I told him to calm down and let me do my job, that by the time I'd finished my meal the restaurant would be full, which it was, and then I left, bought some Romanian girls McDonald's and violently "yelled" at one of them to make her understand that she had to pull over and stop stealing. I told her once, I accept, twice, same thing, but the third time, I made her understand that I was going to "fuck her up" and she listened to me anyway. She told me so, and I hoped she'd learned her lesson, because by the third time, she'd no longer be part of this world.

I continued my journey until nightfall and returned to Ciampino where I found a cheap hotel which I booked with a super-friendly hostess. I got a good night's rest and the next morning, I set off around 8 a.m. to wander around Rome, even though I'd seen it all, but this time it was to take control of it.

What I did: I spent the whole day and night zoning in Europe's third most visited city. I rented an electric scooter for the first time in my life. It was crazy, frankly, it goes fast and as I'm a burnt-out head. I nearly broke my head a few times on it. At the same time, I was on the throttle non-stop.

I took the car from Saint-Pierre to the Colosseum, then back to Saint-Pierre. The streetlamps flickered in my presence.

I had decided to take care of my car, and so I went back to Ciampino to call a tow truck, which took my car back to Tiburtina, near a railway station in Rome, to a garage. Then I paid for my car's faulty part, so that it would be repaired the day I decided to continue my journey through Italy.

In the meantime, I headed for the metro once again, and there was a beggar woman with two aggressive dogs she'd trained to bite. She warned me that they were biting, but of course I didn't listen and wanted to pet them as usual without freaking out. I put my hand up to the biggest dog's head to pet him and he growled at me. I ignored his warnings and kept bugging him until he bit my right hand to the bone. My hand was bloody and I, like him, had become aggressive. I threw my blood on his face with my hand and kicked him in the face with my sneakers, not violently, to make him understand who was the master and that I wasn't afraid of him despite his fangs and his bite.

Then I wandered around for four hours on Rome's subways and buses in the direction of Ciampino with my hand full of blood. I was making the sign of the kingdom and that of Baphomet with my right hand, the one that sends the sheep to heaven, and thus separates them from the goats who are sent to hell with my left hand. People on public transport were quite disturbed to see me like this, but nobody worried about me except a bus driver who asked me if I needed any help, which of course I refused.

Arriving four hours later in Ciampino, I stopped at the MacDonald's where my car used to be parked, then ordered three bottles of water which I opened with my mouth, as my right hand was gradually healing, even though it was swollen with, I don't know what infection.

A woman doctor and her daughter accosted me as they were worried about my hand. So we talked a lot in English and Spanish with her daughter. They also arranged for an ambulance to pick me up to disinfect my hand, which was done despite my reluctance. I ended up in a hospital, and since I don't like lying any more, even if I sometimes do, because everything is allowed to me unlike you (it's the principle of monarchy), I said I was a runaway from French psychiatry and wanted all over France.

A doctor came to ask me some analytical questions and I told him my truth, the truth like Einstein's 6-3=6 (basically that everything is the truth). He told me in English that I needed medication and I told him that they could stick it up their ass.

Then I took off in my angel Gabriel crushing the snake T-shirt. The angel who protects the police. I went to the tobacconist's and bought four packs of Lucky Strike. Then I took the train and the cab to the hotel that had welcomed me two days earlier. The receptionist was very happy to see me again, and so was I, so she re-registered me on the hosting server and then I went to my room. I was knocked out, with all the blood I'd lost, so I went straight to sleep.

It was four o'clock in the morning when the police, accompanied by ambulance drivers, knocked on my door. They let me smoke my cigarettes, I gave them my papers and they took me to the emergency room of a student hospital, waiting for me to be admitted to psychiatry. A team of carabinieri (Italian gendarmes) circle around to keep an eye on me and make sure I don't escape.

At the emergency room, a psychiatrist arrived and I called her all the names that are not usually pronounced. I had ALian accomplices who wore Ray Bans like me and freaked her out. The cops were giving me the thumbs-up, as if to say "well done, mate". I was used to this whole universe by now.

During the police rotation, we told each other that we were brothers and that I was their Big Brother, which they proudly asserted. That I was there to protect the innocent, just like them and my team[14] ! They bought me pizzas, I smoked my cigarettes outside and at night I slept in the emergency room on my bed with a roommate tied to the bed. Then the next day, we waited until evening for them to tie me up for six days and shoot me up.

In Italy, psychology isn't the same as in France, and there's a bit less fun to be had when it comes to injections and treatment methods (laughing out loud). Anyway, when I woke up, I was in a psych ward in the middle of Rome. I was waiting for the ambulance to take me back to France, but the ambulance was cancelled every time. For lack of

---

[14] Team: my team, my srabs and my ALiens

means, or rather, a quarrel between the hospitals to avoid
paying the ambulance fees.

So I hung around the hospital for two weeks, hoping to get back to France while being violently medicated, then one day I had an epiphany and found a loophole. A loophole to escape. Wearing shoes without laces and barefoot in the evening around 8pm, while the nurses were in their offices, I climbed a tap and then the roof. I jumped out of the hospital and ran barefoot until I landed in a field.

The staff were after me and I hid in a field behind a bush. They were shouting my name and I was waiting for them to go away anyway, I've always been the king of running away. When they gave up their search, I was looking for a way to get as far away from the hospital as possible. I'm always up against a challenge, so I went along a barbed-wire fence separating the field from the highway. I found the best spot, in short: there was still some barbed wire, but a few "protective" natural branches. This nature that I protect unlike Orion and his fucking Babylonian world. Yes, I'm on Artemis' side, because in Greek mythology, she sends a giant scorpion to kill Orion so that he doesn't wipe out the animals on Earth.

These branches, natural to me, weren't there by chance. So I climbed the fence barefoot and jumped onto the highway. I landed on the tarmac. My legs and feet were bleeding from the barbed wire, and my right heel exploded as I fell.

I crossed the freeway, then its springboard, and landed in a working-class district of Rome. People asked me if I was all right, and I told them I was, that it was just "an accident" and that I was going home so they'd leave me alone and not call the paramedics again.

I made my way to a corner with a guitarist who had some tobacco to roll. I had nothing left, no papers, no ID, no credit cards, no shoes except my black jacket and shorts. He helped me out with a fag, and played me the guitar with Italian songs. A scooter pulled up to ask who I was, and my fellow guitarist told him I was a friend who'd come to have a good time with him.

The scooter driver then left and I stayed until my colleague went home, then I spent my night sleeping on the grass in a field not far from where I'd spent that moment that can only be described as magical.

The next day, I woke up completely frozen, and the worst thing was that I could hear sheep nearby. I limped off in search of them, but couldn't find them. I walked away all banged up and joined the bus then the metro to end up where my car's garage used to be.

In Rome, I had become "Alexander Supertramp", but I wasn't in the cold, not in ALaska, but just the opposite, in the heart of the city, close to the station and the Tiburtina metro station, which you reach by taking line B, like Bertorello. In short, I used to use the garage ashtrays to smoke the boss's cigars and unused cigarettes, I gave my cell phone to the garage to charge and he gave me the keys to my car so I could sleep in it. Frankly, as a bum, I was in the right place, even if walking on hot asphalt in the blazing sun hurt my feet, I had to do it, to fill up my water bottles and rest in my car with its air-conditioning.

My father was taking news and told me I had to find shoes, which I did by asking people sitting on the benches. I came across an Iraqi immigrant, Imad, a fifty-year-old with grey hair and a ponytail, who had fought in the Iraq war. He took me under his wing and gave me a pair of new shoes in my size. Even though he didn't own anything, he gave me everything I needed and taught me all the tricks of the trade, to the point of teaching me that there was an

Order of Malta at the station, which distributed bags of food to the poor every day.

In fact, I only went there once, as everyone gave me everything I wanted in the way of food. I had a florist close to my car, an Egyptian who had no family of his own and who treated me like a son. His name was Alessandro, with a shaved head, in his fifties. Every morning, he bought me breakfast with cappuccino and croissant filled with custard. I was better off than when I had my credit card, and he paid for my meals every lunchtime and evening, kebabs, pizzas and so on. In short, I sometimes ended up with meals for thirty without being hungry, so I gave what I didn't eat to other homeless people.

Each time, I refused all this, but he forced me to accept and I told him "but I have nothing to offer you". He told me he had no family and that I was a good guy who had become his son. He said I was crazy to have come alone to Rome by car, that it was dangerous for me, and of course I told him "yes, yes", not caring that he was worried about me, but caring about the danger.

Then I met a Palestinian, Kalil, a dark-haired man with brown eyes in his thirties, who often helped me out with tobacco, even though he was undocumented and worked for one euro an hour. He had become my brother at heart. The only thing I could spend my bank account on was Uber Eat, so I bought him McDonald's when he was hungry.

After the day, all I did was walk around, scanning the ground for cigarette butts and finding quite a few, in short, I didn't lack for smoke out there and all I really needed was this. Eating was never my thing, except for pasta. I was showering in church and a bastard priest I wanted to go to confession with refused to let me. In my head, I guaranteed he'd pay dearly on Judgment Day, him and his big bastard Porsche.

I went to mass while protecting my wife, the Virgin Mary, and took selfies in churches. Since I'd realized that the father in heaven I was couldn't fuck a woman as primitive as Mother Earth, Camille, my choice was now Mother in heaven, the Virgin, my new Eve. Two weeks on, and I often go to a little square in Tiburtina, where there's a children's park and benches with elderly people with whom I'd become accustomed to raving. Two characters accosted me, one old and one young, and said to me in Italian, "Hi, Alexandre Bertorello born in Toulon on October 29, 1994?" I replied, "Yes, that's me, but how did you know that? They said, "We know a lot about you, Alexandre". They took me by the arm and said "come with us, we're here to protect you". They made me get into their car, they were unmarked cops. They told me I was a good guy, that they weren't taking me to the psychiatric ward. I knew very well that wasn't true, but I pretended to believe them that I was "Lucifer", the tempter who lets others realize their free will, and therefore their sins. We called ourselves brothers and I was their Big Brother.

Unsurprisingly, they took me to the psychiatric ward from which I'd escaped, lying to me H24 and telling me at the outset that I'd be tied up for a few hours before being released. The few hours lasted eight days, with a catheter in my urethra and neuroleptic injections every three hours. Nurses in shifts to keep an eye on me.

There was one super-crazy nurse I adored who was disgusted to see me tied up like that, but we spent our time chatting about all sorts of subjects. I also saw a big asshole orderly who told me "va fan culo", which means "go fuck yourself" in French. While I was strapped in, I looked at him with a death stare and said, in a mixture of Spanish and Italian, "yo va fan culo?" He replied in English, "no, actually, pardon, I apologize".

I had a visit from the head shrink in the morning and one in the afternoon with all those little students I was flirting with with my catheter in the prostate (laughing out loud). D-Day arrived and the Italian ambulance picked me up. They transferred me from the bed to the stretcher, making sure I didn't escape, and then I was strapped into the ambulance in a "Razmoket" diaper in their fucking ambulance. They bought me a chicken triangle sandwich, but wouldn't let me smoke, of course, so I wouldn't escape.

Anyway, my smoking cure had lasted eight days and was still going on. The paramedics, on the other hand, were cool, so it was okay, we talked about Spain, travel and all sorts of other stuff.

Arriving in Ventimiglia, I was delighted to see Pierre de l'Odyssée again at the ambulance opening. Then there was Laura, whom I also really like, and the ambulance driver Jean-Pierre, whom I didn't know at first, but who I actually find super nice. They untied me straight away, they told the Italians "no need with him, he knows us well", so they did. So I got into Henri Guérin's ambulance and headed for the starting point at Les Palmiers 1 with my war general Marc Antoine, who was present on the battlefield.

I was happy to be back and to see the care team again, and I told them that compared to the shrinks in Italy, this was the Balearic Islands. After all, it's called Les Palmiers 1, and not for nothing! (Laughing). I was very happy to see Céline-Aphrodite again, and her big brother Max, Marie, my buddy Saint-Laurent, Aurélien, the little Nicolas, Myriam the tribe's druidess, Marc Zuckerberg and above all my classy Italian doctor, Valentina, who also follows me at the odyssey along with Madame Geneviève, but she's been there since the CMP.

When Valentina arrived on the ward two days after my reinstatement, she immediately got me back into the Odyssey; frankly, I love it too much. So I landed back at the Odyssey, from where I'm writing this third edition, with Pierre, the one who came to get me, the rooster in the Odyssey nurses' henhouse (laughing out loud). With Princess Hélène, my twin sister and heartthrob Magalie, born on October 29 like me too, in short, the whole team that I'll detail in the acknowledgements at the end of this edition.

As far as the patients are concerned, not much has changed: a lot of misery, a lot of unhappy people, a lot of people complaining, but also a lot of happy people, such as Fabienne, an alcoholic colleague with whom we had some great poker nights at the hospital, and Iliès, my buddy with whom I did the 400 knocks. In short, when you're in psychiatry, you feel like you're part of a big family, and the hospital is like a village. With a large park and the real Martin in which to cool off when it gets too hot. We were a good team, because a lot of people come and go in psychology, which enabled me to get to know all kinds of pathological cases, including borderlines like Agathe, a beautiful blonde, blue-eyed goddess whom I dated and whom I mistook in my delirium for the Virgin Mary, for Eve, because she was of the astrological sign Virgo ascending to Cancer. I'd given her a lady of clubs, which she kept with her, because the lady of clubs, whose name is Argine (an anagram of Regina, meaning Queen), is the queen of the King of Clubs, whose name, as I said, is Alexandre. I loved her like crazy, too much to be straight with her. When I got out, I even took an apartment with her in Toulon, but unfortunately the affair didn't last. I'm too crazy to stay with such a straight-laced girl.

What's next for me, especially in 2023, is shaping up wonderfully, especially as during the vacations I'll have the exclusive right to be looked after by Dr Geneviève. What's more, I've made up with Marine, with whom I am now. The Queen of my fairy kingdom, because I know that whatever happens, she'll always be there for me and I'll always be there for her. I love her and I never want to leave her again. She has become my whole World, my Universe. I moved to Saint-Mandrier-Sur-Mer, a nice peninsula opposite Toulon, with my cats that I recently got. Frankly, for me, everything is gradually getting better, thanks in particular to the injection of Abilify. It's a long-acting neuroleptic that keeps me stable without having to take any more medication. Apart from the fact that every 28 days, a nurse from the CMP has to inject me, I have the freedom and security to live a more or less normal life with the woman in my life. I still feel like I've got the sword of Damocles of a manic crisis hanging over my shoulders, but I try to ignore it and go on with my quiet life as a stable bipolar.

Unfortunately for you, my book is coming to an end.
We wish you all the best of luck and thank you very much!

End of the third edition
Remerciements

Many thanks to the caregivers, all my brothers and sisters or father or mother at heart. And to all the staff at Les Palmiers 1: IDE[15] : Myriam the druidess, Athéna (Noémie), her King my big buddy Denis, Marie, the funny IT lady, Marc Zuckerberg, Vincent, my brother Aurélien. A great person Max frérot de ma petite protégée Aphrodite Céline la blonde, mon grand frérot Mathieu l'infirmier et le petit nouveau Mathieu également, lui aide-soignant, le petit Nicolas, mon grand frérot Saint-Laurent, Pierre mon petit préféré avec ses satellites aux oreilles et ses tatouages de dingue, Stéphane, Diego "Maradona, la mano de dios".

AS[16] : Laurence the conventional. Marjorie the pharaoh from Egypt, Eddy a great guy, Eric.

ASH[17] : Fabienne the sweet blonde, Ginette the funny one too and her mystical delusions, and Nacera.

All the staff at Les Palmiers 2, who unfortunately I can't think of except for Stéphane, my future butler, and finally all the staff at L'Odyssée "le poulailler", the service that's open, well almost, given the number of runaways it sometimes keeps closed.

With Nathalie, IDE, as the new super manager: Laureen, the queen of chess (but not of maths, I don't know) Christelle the sweet, charming and caring blonde

---

[15] IDE : State-qualified nurse.

[16] AS: Aide-soignant

[17] ASH: Hospital service agent

nurse too, Pierre the cock of the henhouse "Pierrot mon gosse mon frangin mon poto qui me tient chaud", Rémi my buddy who used to play World Of Warcraft whom I'll probably nickname the Geek because I'm one from time to time too.

Sweet Lysianne, sometimes jaded but whom I adore, Valérie from the night shift whom I insulted on my trip to Rome, but whom I regret. Véronique, a stickler for the rules but a real mother hen, Christian "Dior", all on the night shift, and Magalie, my darling Scorpio twin born on October 29, who worries a little too much about me "peuchère!" when I don't need to.

Virginie, the beautiful blonde ex-military woman who shoots and plays sports like crazy and whom I really adore for her humility, discretion, gentleness, discipline, kindness and above all intelligence. Then there are the orderlies: Virginie, another mother at heart, who's always there when I take offence, Karima from the night shift, the seamstress from the old days, Marina, another Egyptian pharaoh, Audrey, the cool girl with her "Bob Marley, no woman no cry" bag, Annie, "my woman from the abyss", Hélène, my mother at heart too, whom I seriously adore, who's always there when things aren't going well and who rubs shoulders with my grandmother.

The whole pool team[18] : Sandra the beautiful brunette, Emma the Scorpion, who I don't want to put down so I avoid her now, but whom I adore, Virginie the "warrior" and William "serene" - I can't think of the other names either.

---

[18] Pool: Mobile team.

Now it's the turn of the last superheroes, the Odyssée ASH team with Jess, another scorpion, the hard worker, Philippe and his old Volkswagen Golf, which I adore, and his temperament as a really cool and nice guy; Marjorie, the little darling, always there to make my day, and Axel, the new kid on the block, and finally another Céline, but this one crazy like me too.

All this to say that I'm very satisfied with the role of medicine and hospitals.

I'm also very grateful because I know that unfortunately not all patients have access to the kind of care I had.

Without these structures, I don't know what my life would be like, and I probably wouldn't have been able to share this article.

For all these reasons, I'd like to say a big thank you to all my psychiatrists, even if I've had a lot of conflicts with some of them. A huge thank you to my two psychiatrists whom I appreciate very much, with Geneviève who has been with me for several years and is still with me today. Valentina: if you touch her, I'll bite.

Many thanks to the social workers, in particular Mélanie from Odyssée who helped me enormously with my administrative formalities, and another Virginie from social assistance agency 007, as well as to the psychologists and nurses at the Cuers and La Garde CMPs.

Finally, a big thank you to my father, my uncle, my grandmother, my grandfather, my brother Elie, Christiane, a long-time friend of my father's, who took my brother under her wing and brought him to Spain, where he's flourishing.

In short, I'd die if I had to, to protect all those people, since in a way their goal was to save my life.

So mine is to save theirs. I'd also like to give a big thumbs-up to the student nurses and orderlies, who are doing really well. And let's not forget the people in charge of the cafeteria: Ricou, whose first name is Éric, who calls me "Galoupio", and Nathalie, who tries to calm me down when I get confused with the patients.

I also have a great deal of admiration for the various people in charge of the art studio staff activity centers Jean-Marie, Barbara and Sandrine. The great and courageous Christophe, the vegetable garden manager, who has a heart of gold and a magical personality that takes care of the hospital's plants, whatever the season.

Finally, a big thank you to the courageous owners of the animal farm, including Eric, with his iron courage and golden personality, and the sweet and beautiful blonde Valérie, as well as to the managers of the Loulou Gaffre sports complex, and a big thank you to Adeline, manager of the equitherapy center.